I LIKE TO MOVE IT!

PHYSICAL SCIENCE BOOK FOR KIDS

NEWTON'S LAWS OF MOTION

Children's Physics Books

Hawthorn
3rd grade

This Belongs To
PATTI ZIMMERMAN

www.ProfessorBeaver.ca

Published by Speedy Publishing Canada Limited

PROFESSOR
BEAVER
Building Smarter and Brighter Minds

Motion, Momentum and **Acceleration** are all parts of physical science.

When you *dribble*, *pass*, *shoot* and even *score* in basketball, you are using *Sir Isaac Newton's Laws of Motion*.

In this book, learn **Newton's Three Laws of Motion** – using a basketball!

So, let's get started!

Contents

1

Who Was Sir Issac Newton?

Sir Isaac Newton once said that he saw could further than others because he stood on the "shoulders of giants". When modern physicists say that, they are usually referring to him as the giant. Newton was one of the greatest scientists in history. He laid the foundation for modern physics, not just because he discovered the basic laws of nature that guide it, but also because he developed mathematical principles that made later research possible. Inventions and tools we count on in the modern world could not exist without Newton's discoveries.

Who Was He?

Isaac Newton was an Englishman. He was born on Christmas Day in 1642. He spent his early life at school, studying classical literature and mathematics, until his mother pulled him out in the hope of turning him into a farmer. His teachers complained and talked her into letting Isaac go back to school. He excelled, and went to Cambridge University. He worked to pay his bills until he could win a scholarship.

He went on to have a long academic career. He is most famous for his work on the laws of motion, but he first found fame in mathematics and for his study of light. Newton was the first to realize that white light would split into different colors if it went through a prism, and that those colors could turn back into white light if they went through a second prism that joined them together. This proved

that color was a property of light. He also built an improved telescope using several mirrors. This work laid the foundation for much of Albert Einstein's work on the properties of light.

Newton was famous in his own lifetime, and one of his patrons eventually made him head of the London Mint, where English coins were made. It was supposed to be an easy job, but Newton took it seriously and significantly improved its operations and cracked down on counterfeiting. He eventually retired from his work and died at home in 1727. He never married, and he had no children.

What Are Newton's Laws?

Newton's three laws form the foundation of

Most notably, he was the person who realized that light could be split into different colors with a prism

classical mechanics and much of modern physics. His first law says that an object at rest will stay at rest, and an object in motion will stay in motion, unless an external force acts on it. This quality is called inertia. His second law states that the force exerted by an object is equal to its mass times its acceleration. His third law states that every action has an equal and opposite reaction. In other words when you push an object away, an equal force pushes you away from the object. Newton proved all of these principles, or laws, mathematically, and while they do break down in certain situations, they apply to almost everything you experience in everyday life.

2

Newton's First Law and Basketball

Newton's laws form the basis of modern physics. They explain how objects move when something applies force to them. It may seem like they should be complicated, but they are actually quite simple. Let's see how Newton's First Law of motion works by looking at how a basketball bounces and flies during a game.

What Is The First Law?

The First Law of motion is so simple that it might seem obvious, but every scientists knows that even something that looks obvious still needs to be proved. Newton used a lot of math to explain his law, but the simplest way to say it

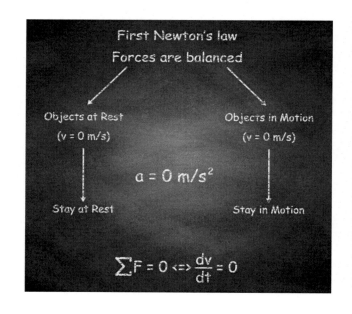

This is called inertia. Everything has inertia, from people, to cars, to basketballs. If you want to get a feel for how inertia works, pick up your basketball!

is that an object that isn't moving won't start to move unless something pushes it, while an object that is moving will keep moving in the same direction and at the same speed until something forces it to stop, change its speed, or change its direction.

Dropping the Ball

The simplest thing that you can do with a basketball is drop it. When you let go of the ball without pushing it down at the same time, it falls to the ground. When it hits the ground, it might bounce back up. That will repeat a couple of times until the ball stops moving.

Newton's law tells us that some force is acting on the ball. If that was not the case, the ball would simply float in the air. Anyone who has ever dropped a basketball knows that doesn't happen. So, what force is it?

In this case, gravity is the force that pulls the ball. If you took a basketball into outer space, where the force of gravity is so weak that it can't do anything, the ball really would float instead of falling.

This may seem obvious, but it was a big deal when Newton

Newton's law tells us that some force is acting on the ball... gravity is the force that pulls the ball

discovered it. Before he came along, most people believed Aristotle's explanation. Aristotle was a Greek who thought that every object had a natural place in the world, and it would always try to get there. He thought that rocks fell because

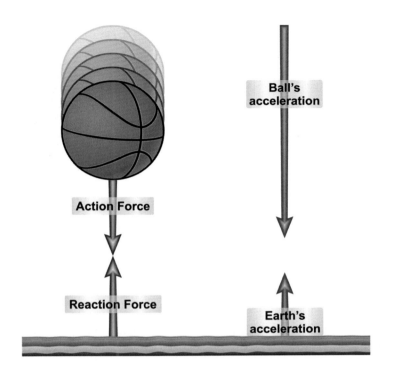

they wanted to be on the ground, while smoke floated because it wanted to be in the air. When Newton showed that inertia was a natural and predictable process, people realized that they could predict how objects would move in different situations and use that knowledge to create machines.

Passing the Ball

Think of two players passing a basketball. One of them throws the ball to the other. This provides the force that gets the ball moving in the first place. The other player might catch it, or he might miss. If he misses, the ball will keep going until it hits the ground or runs into a wall. Either way, the ball will bounce, roll, and eventually stop, and this means there are forces at work on it.

The simplest case is when the second player catches the ball. The player pushes his hands against the ball while gripping it. The pushing exerts force, and it's enough to overcome the ball's

inertial force that it got when the first player threw it. If the second player exerts the right amount of force, the ball stops moving in his hands. If he uses too much force, the ball bounces off his hands and keeps moving  in a new direction. The force overcame the ball's inertia, but added new force which gave the ball a new inertial force. This illustrates something very important. Inertia fights against any change to speed or direction, not just against stopping or starting.

If the second player misses the ball, things get a little more complicated. If the ball keeps going until it hits a wall, the wall will apply some force to the ball, and the ball will respond by continuing in a new direction. However, the wall isn't the only force at work. Gravity still applies, so the ball will generally go towards the ground. It might take a few bounces, but it will finally come to rest on the ground. If the ball doesn't hit a wall, gravity will make sure that it ends up on the ground anyway. This isn't very different from just dropping the ball. The thrown ball has sideways motion and inertial energy, and downwards motion caused by the force of gravity.

Inertia fights against any change to speed or direction, not just against stopping or starting.

23

Making a Shot

Inertial energy and the force of gravity apply to almost everything that a basketball does during the game. Let's look at how the ball moves as a player tries to score and see how Newton's First Law applies.

He pushes the ball down, which combines with gravity to overcome its inertia. It hits the floor, and the floor pushes back. That overcomes its inertia once more...

The player needs to get the ball down the court, so he starts dribbling. He pushes the ball down, which combines with gravity to overcome its inertia. It hits the floor, and the floor pushes back. That overcomes its inertia once more, and sends the ball back to the player's hand. He keeps doing that until he's in position to shoot for the basket.

Our player takes the shot, using his own force to beat inertia. He hits the rim or the backboard. They hit back, and overcome the ball's inertia to send it flying in a new direction. The ball also exerted some force on the rim, but the rim stayed in place because the ball didn't have enough force to overcome the rim's inertia.

The player gets the ball again and takes another shot. This one arcs up high, but it comes down again because gravity is applying force to it. The ball goes through the basket—nothing but net!—and our player scores. The ball hits the ground exactly as it did when the player was dribbling, bounces up because the floor exerts force on it, and keeps on bouncing until eventually comes to a stop or someone grabs it. If someone wants to move the ball again, they'll have to overcome its inertia.

3

Newton's Second Law and Basketball

What is The Second Law?

Newton's Second Law of motion predicts how quickly an object will change its direction or speed in response to something pushing it. The rate that it changes is called the object's acceleration, while the thing that is pushing it is called the force. The object's mass is also important, and it measures how much stuff is being pushed. This isn't quite the same as measuring how big it is, since something

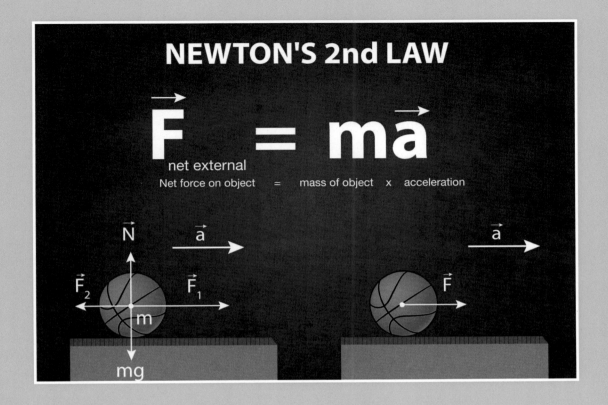

that is very small and very dense will have a lot of mass, while something that is big but has a lot of empty space, such as a basketball, will have much less mass. We can express the law in an equation that says that force is equal to mass times acceleration.

Dribbling

Imagine yourself dribbling a basketball down the court. When you push on the ball, it heads towards the ground. It hits the ground, and then it bounces back up. The harder you hit the ball towards the ground, the faster it will go. Newton's law explains exactly what is going on when this happens.

Think back to the equation, force equals mass times acceleration. If you know any two of those variables, you can solve the equation to get the third. In this case, you will always know what the basketball's mass is. That value won't change unless you change the ball. That means that if you know how much force you are putting on the ball, you can figure out how fast it will head towards the ground. If you know how fast it is going, you can find out how much force acted on it.

if you know how much force you are putting on the ball, you can figure out how fast it will head towards the ground

When the ball goes down, there are two forces at work. The first is gravity. This pulls things towards the ground at a constant rate. The second force comes from you. When you push the ball towards the ground, you are applying force to it. You have to add both of these forces together to get the total force that is acting on the ball. Once you do that, all it takes is a

little bit of math to find out how fast the ball is going.

Making a Pass

Working that equation is useful if you're just curious about how fast you can move a ball, but it also has some practical value. Imagine that you're playing basketball, and you need to pass the ball to your friend. You know that you want to get the ball moving as fast as possible, to make sure that the other team can't catch it before your friend does. On the other hand, he might miss the ball if it is going too fast.

If you did some testing before the game, you could find out just how fast the ball could go before your friend would miss it. This isn't the same as knowing how much acceleration the ball should have, since acceleration refers to how quickly the speed will change, but a little bit of math can give you the maximum acceptable acceleration if you do know the maximum speed. Do the math, and you have one of the variables for your equation.

You also know the mass of the basketball, because that never changes.

So now you have everything that you need to know to figure out how hard to throw the ball. Multiply the mass of the ball with the ideal acceleration. This will give you the force that you should use when you pass the ball. If you can figure out a way to throw it exactly that hard, you'll have the perfect pass. Uh, if you throw it in the right direction.

Multiply the mass of the ball with the ideal acceleration. This will give you the force that you should use when you pass the ball.

Failed Interceptions

What happens if multiple forces try to push the ball in different directions? Suppose you're trying to pass the ball. Someone on the other team tries to catch it, but all he manages to do is slap it back toward you.

In this case, the forces will largely work against each other. When you throw the ball, it has some amount of force behind it. If the other person hits it with the same amount of force in exactly the opposite direction, those forces will cancel each other and gravity will pull the ball toward the floor. If he hits it with more force, the ball will head back towards you, with the force greater than what you supplied. The ball will come toward you, but probably more slowly than when you threw it.

When you throw the ball, it has some amount of force behind it. If the other person hits it with the same amount of force in exactly the opposite direction, those forces will cancel each other and gravity will pull the ball toward the floor.

Of course, most people don't throw perfectly straight. Suppose that you throw the ball forward and a little bit to your left. The opponent hits it back toward you, but he also gives it a push to his right (your left). The forward and backward forces will cancel out as they did before, but that still leaves the forces sending the ball to your left, plus gravity. The ball will head not back to you, but to your left and probably out of bounds. This shows that you have to keep track of the forces going in each direction separately (the vectors) if you want to predict where the ball will go.

Newton's Third Law and Basketball

If you want to understand motion, you need to take a look at Newton's laws. There are three of them, and the Third Law is the most complicated. It's also one of the most important laws in all of physics. Fortunately, it is still fairly simple to understand as long as you keep the other two laws in mind.

What Is The Third Law?

Newton's Third Law states that every action has an equal and opposite reaction. If you push on something, it will push back in the opposite direction with exactly as much force as you applied to it. This is true

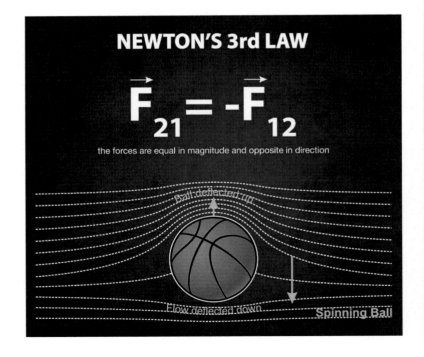

NEWTON'S 3rd LAW

$$\vec{F}_{21} = -\vec{F}_{12}$$

the forces are equal in magnitude and opposite in direction

Ball deflected up

Flow deflected down

Spinning Ball

Newton's third law states that every action has an equal and opposite reaction. If you push on something, it will push back in the opposite direction with exactly as much force as you applied to it.

for almost every object in the universe, even things like floors and walls that seem like they can't push anything. It's easy to see how it works if you look at a basketball.

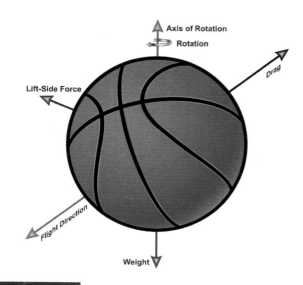

Bouncing Balls

Picture yourself dribbling a basketball on the court. When the ball hits the ground, it bounces back up into the air. However, Newton's First Law tells us that the ball should only be changing its direction if another force acts on it. This seems like a problem, but the Third Law explains what is happening.

When the ball hits the floor, it applies some downward force to it. At the same time, the floor applies an equal force to the ball, pushing up instead of down. This allows the ball to change its direction and start going up again without violating the other laws of motion. This is the Third Law's equal and opposite reaction.

This also happens when the ball returns to your hand. When the ball hits your hand, it applies force to it. Even if you hold your hand perfectly still and don't try to push down on the ball, your hand will still exert a downward force when the ball hits it, equal to the ball's upward force. That will cause the ball to go back down toward the floor again.

It may seem like the ball could keep bouncing forever,

If the ball hits the ground at an angle, some of the force pushes it left or right instead of up...

but anyone who has bounced a ball knows that it will stop moving at some point. That happens because there are a lot of different forces acting on the ball. For example, the ball needs to push air out of the way as it moves. When that happens, the ball applies force to the air, and the air pushes back. Air is very light, so the force isn't strong enough to make the ball change direction, but it will slow it down a little. If the ball hits the ground at an angle, some of the force pushes it left or right instead of up. That will keep happening, and the force gets divided each time the ball hits the ground, until it doesn't have enough force to get into the air again.

Running Down The Court

You can only move because of what Newton's Third Law describes. Imagine yourself running down the court on your way to score a basket. When your foot hits the floor, it is applying force in exactly the same way as the bouncing ball. The floor pushes back, which causes your foot to stop moving down. If you push the floor backwards, as you do when you run, the floor pushes you forward at the same time.

If this didn't happen, you would have a very hard time moving. Your foot would still hit the floor, but there wouldn't be any force that could overcome its inertia and cause it to stop going down. Your foot would break through the floor and keep going until something else happened to stop it.

Dunking

Suppose that you have finally reached the other end of the court and you want to make a slam dunk. You start off with a jump, which works just like running. Your feet put a lot of force into the floor, and the floor pushes back on you with the same amount of force, which sends you up into the air.

However, you probably aren't jumping straight up. You also want to move forward at the same time. When you jump forward, your feet are pushing diagonally, both down and behind you. Since the floor needs to exert force in the opposite direction, it pushes you up and forward at the same time.

Once you're in the air, you push down on the ball to get it through the hoop. This will technically put a little bit of upward force on you, but it's too small to matter. Remember that force is equal to mass times

Remember that force is equal to mass times acceleration, and that a basketball has very little mass...

acceleration, and that a basketball has very little mass. That's why you can get the ball to move very quickly with relatively little force. Since you have a lot of mass compared to the ball, the force that it applies on you when you dunk it won't make you move more than a little.

Catching the Ball

Scoring is important, but there are also times when you need to pass and catch the ball if you want to win. When you make a catch, you need to hold the ball tightly to make it stop moving. If you don't, it will just bounce out of your hands. Newton's Third Law explains why that happens.

The ball applies force to your hands when it hits them, and the equal and opposite reaction pushes the ball back away from you. When you hold the ball tightly, your hands apply other forces to it from the sides. If those forces are strong enough, they overcome the force that wants to push the ball out of your hands and you hang on to the ball.

This is why it is easier to catch the ball with two hands instead of one. The ball applies force to both hands, and both hands push back and inward. If your hands are pushing in toward the center of the ball, then a lot of their forces will cancel out. The force coming from the left hand stops the reaction that pushes the ball towards it, and the right hand's force does the same from the other side. If your hands don't apply exactly the same amount of force in exactly opposite directions, there will be a little bit left over. That might make the ball start to slip out of your hands, but friction, gravity, and other minor forces can be enough to help you hang on t the ball.

NOW you know how basketball and Newton's Laws work together

Made in the USA
Lexington, KY
25 March 2018